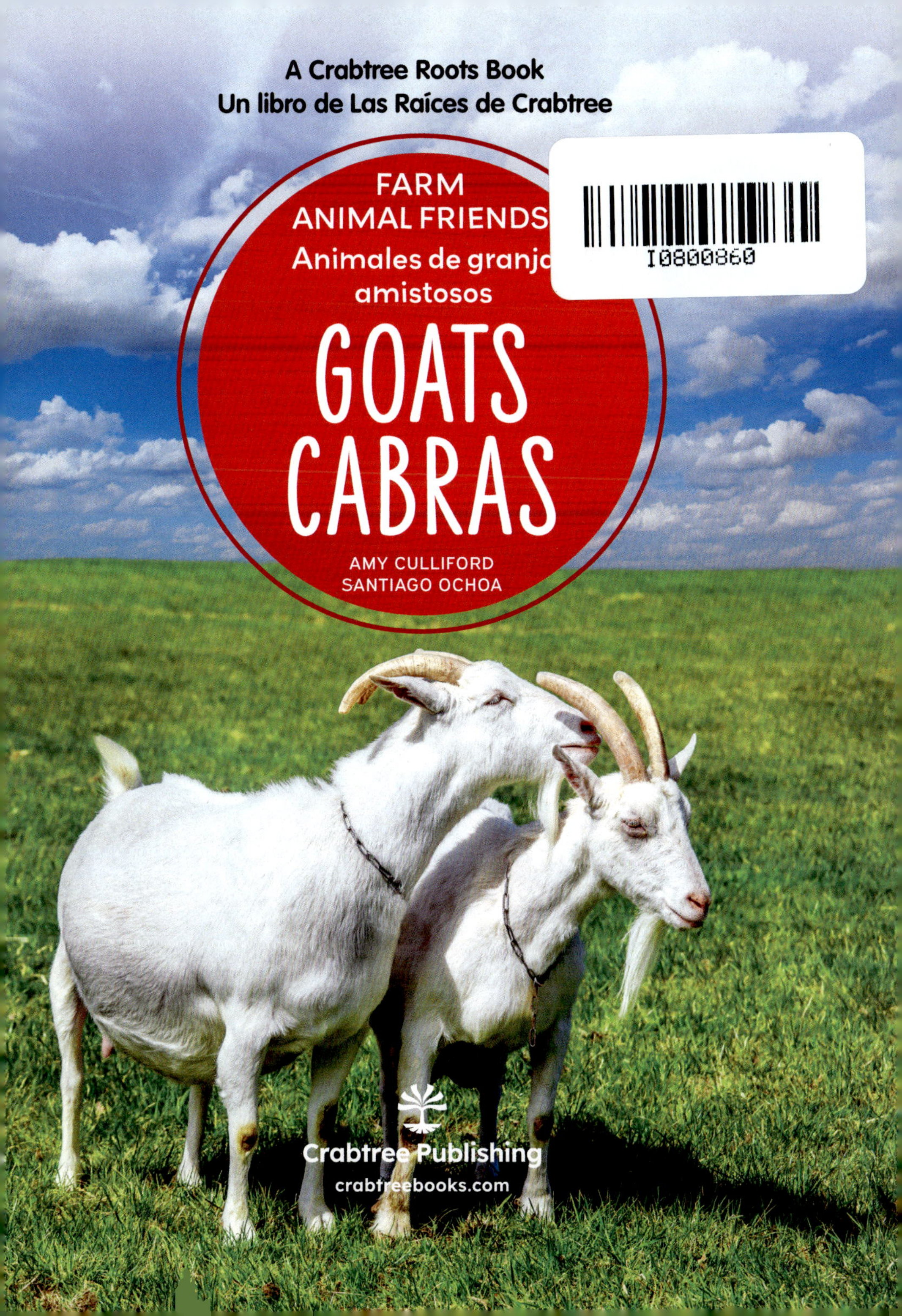

A Crabtree Roots Book
Un libro de Las Raíces de Crabtree

FARM ANIMAL FRIENDS
Animales de granja amistosos

GOATS
CABRAS

AMY CULLIFORD
SANTIAGO OCHOA

Crabtree Publishing
crabtreebooks.com

School-to-Home Support for Caregivers and Teachers

This book helps children grow by letting them practice reading. Here are a few guiding questions to help the reader with building his or her comprehension skills. Possible answers appear here in red.

Before Reading:

- What do I think this book is about?
  - *This book is about goats.*
  - *This book is about goats on farms.*

- What do I want to learn about this topic?
  - *I want to learn what goats eat.*
  - *I want to learn what colors a goat can be.*

During Reading:

- I wonder why...
  - *I wonder why goats like to eat hay.*
  - *I wonder why goats like to jump.*

- What have I learned so far?
  - *I have learned that goats can be different colors.*
  - *I have learned that some goats make milk.*

After Reading:

- What details did I learn about this topic?
  - *I have learned that goats can be white or brown.*
  - *I have learned that goats like to eat hay.*

- Read the book again and look for the vocabulary words.
  - *I see the word **hay** on page 8 and the word **milk** on page 10. The other vocabulary words are found on page 14.*

This is a **goat**.

Esta es una **cabra**.

Some goats are white.

Algunas cabras son blancas.

Some goats are brown.

Algunas cabras son cafés.

Goats like to eat **hay**.

A las cabras les gusta comer **heno**.

Some goats make **milk**.

Algunas cabras producen **leche**.

All goats like to jump!

¡A todas las cabras les gusta saltar!

Words to Know
Palabras para aprender

goat
cabra

hay
heno

milk
leche

26 Words

This is a **goat**.
Some goats are white.
Some goats are brown.
Goats like to eat **hay**.
Some goats make **milk**.
All goats like to jump!

30 palabras

Esta es una **cabra**.
Algunas cabras son blancas.
Algunas cabras son cafés.
A las cabras les gusta comer **heno**.
Algunas cabras producen **leche**.
¡A todas las cabras les gusta saltar!

FARM ANIMAL FRIENDS
Animales de granja amistosos

GOATS
CABRAS

Written by: Amy Culliford

Designed by: Rhea Wallace

Series Development: James Earley

Proofreader: Kathy Middleton

Educational Consultant: Christina Lemke M.Ed.

Photographs:
Shutterstock: fs24: cover (tl); Nataliia Melnychuk: cover (tr); oorka: cover (b); 2xSamara.com: p. 1; Khort Esther Tatiana: p. 3, 14; Anton Havelaar: p. 4; Gelphi: p. 7; Janis Petranis: p. 9, 14; DenysR: p. 10-11, 14; Grigorita Ko: p.13

Crabtree Publishing

crabtreebooks.com 800-387-7650

Printed in Canada/042023/CPC20230419

Published in Canada
Crabtree Publishing
616 Welland Ave.
St. Catharines, Ontario
L2M 5V6

Published in the United States
Crabtree Publishing
347 Fifth Avenue,
Suite 1402-145
New York, NY, 10016

Library and Archives Canada Cataloguing in Publication
Available at the Library and Archives Canada

Library of Congress Cataloging-in-Publication Data
Available at the Library of Congress

Paperback: 9781039624450
Ebook: 9781039625297
Epub: 9781039624870